off.

YOUR DIGITAL DETOX
FOR A BETTER LIFE

For Ellie and Finn,
the two very best reasons
for logging off

First published in Great Britain in 2018
by Octopus Publishing Group Ltd,
Carmelite House, 50 Victoria
Embankment, London EC4Y 0DZ
www.octopusbooks.co.uk

Library of Congress Control Number:
2017949414

ISBN: 978-1-4197-3086-3
eISBN: 978-1-68335-299-0

Text copyright © 2018 Tanya Goodin
Design and Layout © 2018 Octopus
Publishing Group Ltd
Cover © 2018 Abrams

Photography credits:
Alamy Stock Photo: 108 Saran Poroong.
Unsplash: 4 Gaelle Marcel; 12 Chris
Chondrogiannis; 14 Austin Neill; 16
elizabeth lies; 18 Janko Ferlic; 20 Krista
Mangulsone; 22 Oskar Krawczyk; 24
Brooke Lark; 26 Matthew Kane; 28
Loic Djim; 30 Zachary Staines; 32
Thomas Kelley; 34 Muhammed Kara;
36 Luis Dávila; 38 Patrick Tomasso; 40
Dmitri Popov; 42 Florian Klauer; 45
Annie Spratt; 46 Gaelle Marcel; 49
Andre Hunter; 50 Ben White; 52 Sweet
Ice Cream Photography; 54 Annie
Spratt; 56 Mariona Campmany; 58
Benjamin Combs; 60 Tolga Kilinc; 63
Gili Benita; 64 Brooke Cagle; 67
quentin lagache; 68 Alexandre
Chambon; 71 paul itkin; 72 Tim Gouw;
74 Timon Studler; 77 Kristina Flour; 78
NordWood Themes; 81 Greg Rakozy; 82
adrian; 84 Semih Aydın; 87 Simson
Petrol; 88 Chad Madden; 90 Aidan
Meyer; 92 Anh Phan; 95 Federica
Campanaro; 96 photo-nic.co.uk nic; 98
Evan Kirby; 100 Elena Ferrer; 102 Greg
Raines; 105 Clarisse Meyer; 106 Andrey
Larin; 110 Ivan Slade.

Printed and bound in China
10 9 8 7 6 5 4 3 2 1

Abrams Image books are available at
special discounts when purchased in
quantity for premiums and promotions
as well as fundraising or educational
use. Special editions can also be created
to specification. For details, contact
specialsales@abramsbooks.com or the
address below.

ABRAMS The Art of Books
195 Broadway, New York, NY 10007
abramsbooks.com

off.

YOUR DIGITAL DETOX
FOR A BETTER LIFE

TANYA GOODIN

ABRAMS IMAGE, NEW YORK

CONTENTS

HOW TO USE THIS BOOK

Email. Tweet. Facebook.
Snapchat. Instagram. Message.
Call. Browse. Play. Date. Shoot.
Film. Record. Blog. Note.

Walk down any street, stroll through any park, step into any bar, café, or restaurant and everyone is hunched over their mobile devices. No one talking, all glued to their screens. The technology designed to connect and enable us has begun to do the opposite.

This book will give you your life back! It will free up hours of your time to rediscover the things you love, by helping you to develop a healthy relationship with your digital devices.

A digital detox isn't about hurling your screens into a trash can and reverting to a tech-free way of life. It's not about giving up the digital world altogether. A digital detox is about learning to live with technology in a way that's healthy. It's about *balance.*

So how can we regain some balance in our lives? How can we rediscover the world outside our smartphones and tablets, while still making the most of everything the digital world has to offer?

In this book you'll find some practical tips and tricks I've developed from my personal experience to stop screens from taking over your life. These involve a range of techniques, prompts, and suggestions to unplug, recharge, find time, de-stress, and regain some peace in our wired world.

Whether you're frazzled due to a 24/7 email habit, exhausted from poor sleep, unhappy about family time losing out to screen time, aware that your attention span is shot to pieces, anxious if you're even momentarily separated from your phone, or in a bad mood every time you're on social media—this book is for you.

It's not that the digital world is bad, it's almost that it's too good. It's why everywhere you look everyone is on their phones, *all* the time—but this is affecting our physical and mental health. We've introduced tiny tyrants into our pockets that demand constant attention. We need help to escape their clutches and put them back where they belong.

In Set Your Boundaries you'll learn how to draw simple and workable boundaries based around time and place, to set limits on your time online.

Go with the Flow introduces you to absorbing mindfulness-based activities that will rest your screen-frazzled brain and help you to rebuild your attention span.

Get Back to Nature encourages you to get outside, away from screens, and discover the healing power of nature to regenerate and restore.

Tame Your Triggers looks at the various ways the online world can hook us back in when we're trying to stay offline, and how to combat them.

Choose Analog offers some screen-free activities as better alternatives for screen-based ones.

Reconnect will inspire you to disconnect from superficial online relationships and strengthen your real-world ones.

You may be anxious at the thought of

putting down your phone or being without it for any period of time. You're not alone! But my experience with helping people do a digital detox is that the anticipation is always worse than the reality. Everyone who has tried these techniques has found them far easier and far more rewarding than they thought they would.

At the digital detox retreats I run, we know from our pre– and post–digital detox surveys that the happiness levels of our guests are almost double by the end of their stay. What's more, most people make permanent changes in their screen habits after attending. One woman now puts her phone in a drawer when her children come home from school, another man no longer answers work email after 7pm at night. Others have decided to use only their landline in the evenings, or to swap out their SIM card into a non-smartphone for holidays, or even to make weekends entirely screen-free. They may be small changes, but they have a very big impact.

As you work your way through the book

or dip in and out of it, you'll become aware of your particular personal challenges around screens, and gain an understanding of what will help you overcome them. And as you discover for yourself the benefits of logging off, through improved sleep, focus, productivity, and mood, I know you'll be inspired to do more and keep going.

I guarantee that within these pages there will be something that works for you. Start your digital detox today!

Tanya Goodin

SET YOUR BOUNDARIES

Regaining balance from any addiction starts with setting boundaries. It's not that we're using screens at all that's the problem, it's that we're using them *without limits*. Our screens are our constant companions all day and night, at work and at play, when we're with friends and when we're alone. There's no respite. No wonder our brains are frazzled. How can we ever switch off?

The simplest boundaries to set relate to time and place. Consider your lifestyle and decide where screens simply don't belong. Then look at the times when you should be setting them down. Start by setting small workable limits and work up to more significant lines in the sand. Even just one or two "no-go" times and places will reduce your screen overuse, and free up a surprising amount of time to do the things you really enjoy.

Here are some boundary suggestions to get you started.

1. Wake Up

—

Our smartphones have invaded our bedrooms. They're the first thing we see in the morning and the last thing we see at night. With their blue-light-emitting screens, they suppress our melatonin levels (the chemical that sets our biological clock), which hinders our ability to get a good nights' sleep.

So, buy an alarm clock.

We've become used to relying on our devices' built-in applications to wake up. Using an alarm clock instead is your single best weapon against the tide of technology wreaking havoc on your sleep schedule, leaving you more rested and energetic. Until you've bought that all-important alarm, leave your phone outside your door so you can hear the phone alarm without having your device in your bedroom.

—

2. Screen Scheduling

—

We need to reestablish some rules in our "always-on" culture, about when work stops and when play begins, for our physical and our mental health.

A time boundary is set when you draw the line between work and play, when you're "on" and when you're "off." Some goals you might set:

> Switch devices off at 10pm.

> No email after 7pm.

> Screen-free Sundays to enjoy quality time with family or friends.

> Digital Sabbaths (no logging on over the weekends). To give yourself a fighting chance, plan something else to do during the time when you've set your time boundary. And put your screens somewhere out of sight so that you don't inadvertently get drawn into picking them up or turning them back on.

—

*And the night
shall be filled
with music,
And the cares,
that infest the day,
Shall fold their
tents, like the Arabs,
And as silently
steal away.*

HENRY WADSWORTH LONGFELLOW

3. Before Bed

—

For many of us there's no winding-down time at all before we nod off. And simply switching off our phones and hoping we can shut down at the same speed is not the answer.

Even if you can't ban your phone from your bedroom entirely, one really useful boundary to establish is the last time at night that you check your phone or tablet.

—

4. Unplugged

—

The first time I stepped out without my phone I felt anxious. I hadn't been anywhere without it for such a long time, so I kept patting my pocket reflexively to check whether it was still there. This weird behavior even has a name: "nomophobia"—the fear of being without your phone.

Start small, with just an excursion to the corner shop. Think of it as exercising your digital detox muscle: you have to work out how to engage it before you can start the heavy lifting. Before long you'll find you can go for longer and longer periods without being tethered to your phone, without panicking or worrying.

—

5. Phone-Free Food

—

How many of us complain about friends, family, and loved ones checking their phones while eating with us? Yet many of us are guilty of the same offense.

<u>Start enjoying quality time and food together.</u>

Whether it's snatching a sandwich by yourself or enjoying a longer meal with someone else, resolve to keep your phone tucked away, hidden, and out of sight. Make your meal moments mini–digital detox moments. Savor and enjoy what you're eating, and relish every mouthful free from screen distractions.

—

6. Bathroom Ban

—

W hat is it about our addiction to our phones that means we can't leave them behind, even when we take a bath? Why can't we just relax and enjoy a long soak? What is so urgent that it can't wait?

Try banishing your smartphone from bathtime for a week. Pause, be mindful, and enjoy the experience. You really don't *need* to use this time to keep up-to-date on social media, messages, or the news. Just lie back and enjoy.

Take time to remind yourself how relaxing a few minutes without your phone can be.

—

7. Track Tech Time

—

$\mathbf{T}$ry for one day to make a note of every
time you pick up your phone and
when you put it down again. With some
research showing we pick up our phones
up to 150 times a day, just logging it all may
be a challenge!

Each time you make a note (even just a
mental one) of when you check your phone,
notice how long it's been *since the last time*
you checked it. You'll quickly get a sense of
how much time in your day you're making
available to focus on other activities—and
how long you can actually go before you get
the urge to pick up your phone.

This exercise will give you an idea of
how much time your phone habit eats up.
You might well find yourself shocked at all
those wasted minutes (and hours).

—

8. Put Your Phone in Its Place

—

1. Find a box or basket big enough to hold all the smartphones in your household. Make sure whatever you choose makes it impossible to see the phones once they are inside (removing temptation).

2. Agree on a central location where the container will be kept. Perhaps the hallway right where everyone comes in, or just outside the kitchen.

3. Discuss with everyone in the household what the rules are for when phones need to be stowed here. Is it as soon as anyone enters the house? Overnight? During family meals? Only on a specified phone-free day of the week?

4. Set a test period when you can try out the phone container and see how it's working for you.

5. Tweak the plan to maximize chances of sticking to it.

6. Get going!

—

GO WITH
THE FLOW

One study estimates that we tap, swipe, and click on our devices an average of 2,617 times a day. Yet another, that we consume more than five times as much information a day than we did in 1986.

The result of this constant connectivity and deluge of information is rising rates of burnout and stress, and rapidly deteriorating concentration. One piece of research even claims our human concentration span is now less than that of a goldfish!

The ideal activities to recharge and restore your screen-addled brain are those in which you can enter a state of "flow"—a meditative state in which your breathing and heart rate slow down considerably.

Flow occurs when you become totally absorbed in what you're doing such that your brain simply can't be distracted by anything else. Time just seems to fly by and you may even lose track of it completely.

To find the perfect "unplugged" pursuit, try out a range of activities that require all your focus, and preferably both your hands—so you can't juggle your phone while doing it. This section has a few suggestions.

1. Mindful Coloring

—

Why are coloring books so popular? Probably because coloring in an intricate and detailed pattern has been found to be one of the best activities to relax with.

Unlike more physical activities that get you into a state of flow, such as surfing or yoga, coloring requires very little skill, so we can all do it. It also harks back to our childhoods, so it's evocative and nostalgic—and it's incredibly satisfying when you complete a difficult design.

A creative outlet is important when your brain is moving at break-neck speed

for most of the day. Coloring in beautiful illustrations not only takes you on a trip down memory lane but also gives your brain a well-earned rest.

Coloring is particularly good if you find it hard to relax and switch off; altering the brainwaves from alpha to beta (which occurs when you're in flow) facilitates deep sleep, so it's great to do to unwind before bed for a good night's sleep.

But coloring is fantastic for clearing the head at any time of day, even if done in just 10- or 15-minute bursts. With repeated coloring sessions you'll soon find you can focus for longer when doing other activities too.

—

2. Turn the Page

—

When was the last time you got lost in a book? Really deeply immersed, turning the pages hypnotically and lifting your head only to find with surprise that most of the day has gone?

One of the casualties of our over-dependence on screens is our relationship with reading. When we're used to snatching sound bites of news and entertainment here and there from online news sites and social media, it's hard to stay focused on reading long enough to get drawn into a good book.

If reading for long periods of time is something that you're struggling with, start by setting a small challenge of reading for just six minutes a day. Read before bed and it'll help with sleep too.

—

3. Complete a Puzzle

—

S martphones are constant distractions. Their intrusive notifications and hard-to-ignore alert sounds mean that we're developing what's known as "monkey brain"—rapid mental darting from one thing to another, between what's happening on our screens and what's actually going on in our lives—and it's completely eroding our concentration and focus.

Remember the joy of jigsaw puzzles from your childhood? They're the perfect activity to get lost in to recharge your brain.

Choose a puzzle that has a complex design, preferably with more than one thousand pieces. The idea is to become completely absorbed in finding and fitting all the tiny pieces. Time will fly by.

—

Journal writing is a voyage to the interior.

CHRISTINA BALDWIN

4. Keep a Journal

———

Scientists are discovering that there appears to be a special relationship between the brain and the hand: writing by hand stimulates a unique neural circuit that simply isn't activated by typing. Some research even suggests that the act of writing by hand may help us to learn better and be able to commit something to memory much more easily than by typing it.

However, writing in a journal offers more than just the benefits associated with writing by hand. Setting down your thoughts and reflecting on your day encourages you to be more mindful and notice what's going on in your life.

Journaling can be as brief or as time intensive as you want it to be—a five-minute exercise in closing the day by jotting down a few thoughts to help you drift off to sleep, or a longer "voyage to the interior." Either way, journaling delivers the most benefits when you commit to it as a daily practice. Start by journaling every day for a week and see how you do.

———

5. Sew Something

—

In, out, in, out, in, out...
The steady movement of a sewing needle piercing its way through fabric can be a hypnotic and meditative experience.

Find a button that's fallen off, a hem that needs fixing, or an item that needs a name tag and settle down in a quiet corner with a needle and thread.

A mere five minutes of sewing will slow down your breathing and reduce your stress levels.

As a bonus, sewing over time will improve your hand-eye coordination *and* smarten up your wardrobe! Knitting and crocheting are also good activities to try, with similar repetitive movements to help you enter a state of flow.

—

6. Cook

—

1. Dig out an old recipe that you love. Make sure it involves something that will really absorb you, where you can dig in and use your hands—rolling out pastry, cutting biscuits, and making pasta dough from scratch are good examples of this.

2. Clear the kitchen of digital devices and distractions, and lay out all the ingredients and utensils.

3. Focus as you measure out the ingredients.

4. Read the instructions carefully and absorb yourself in the step-by-step process.

5. Really notice the sensations on your hands as you're handling the ingredients and mixing them together.

6. Appreciate the smell and look of your creation as it starts to come together.

7. Enjoy!

—

7. Move

—

Being immersed in the digital world inevitably involves a lack of physical movement. We're stuck at our desks all day and when we're not we're glued to our phones, often completely immobile. Moving physically is a great way to get out of our heads and into our bodies, resting our brains in the process.

Any form of mindful movement is a good way to get into the flow state. Yoga is particularly good for developing concentration because the effort required to get into some of the harder poses demands complete focus. Yoga's emphasis on breathing also helps you to enter a meditative and restful state.

But there are many other types of mindful movement you can try; Pilates, dancing, surfing, or running—all of these require practice and skill to master and perfect. And all of them can help you get into the zone that will help you recharge your brain.

Try as many different types of mindful movement as you can until you find one that works for you.

—

8. Memorize a Poem

—

You can probably still remember a special poem you learned as a child. See if you can recall it now. Do the words come flooding back when you concentrate? What images and sensations do they bring back for you?

Committing something to memory requires time and focus, but it is extremely satisfying when you achieve it.

Find a poem that appeals to you and give yourself the challenge of memorizing it. As you repeat the words back and forth, testing yourself to see how much you've managed to retain, you'll find yourself entering a mindful state—all that matters are the words in the poem and whether you've captured them.

At the end you'll have some beautiful words flowing around in your head that you can bring to mind whenever you want. You could also try memorizing an excerpt from your favorite play or book, if that's more your style.

—

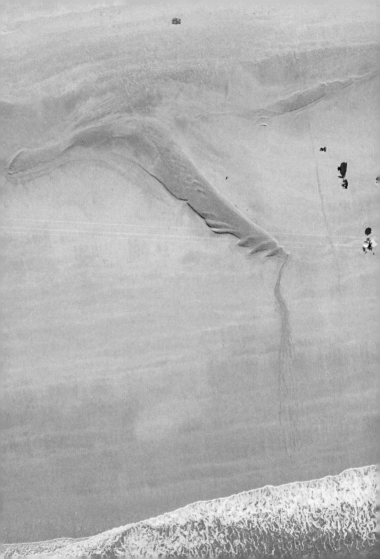

GET BACK
TO NATURE

When we decide to do a digital detox we're not just making a decision to switch off; we're also choosing new ways to spend our time. Reconnecting with nature is one of the very best things to make time for each day.

Keeping one foot always in the digital world means we're losing our valuable connection with the natural world. And yet we know so much about how nature heals and nurtures us. For both physical and mental health, getting out in nature is inspiring and regenerative.

In adults, even a quick glimpse of nature has been proven to improve concentration and productivity. And in children, walking in the park has been shown to decrease symptoms of ADHD. Exposure to nature has even been linked to the improved functioning of our immune systems.

Scientists have found that ample time spent in natural light is key to maintaining healthy circadian rhythms in the body—

the biological cycles that regulate our sleep, mood, hormones, and stress levels. How many more reasons do you need to get away from screens and go outside? This section has some ideas on how you can reconnect with nature.

1. Wander

—

The average person in a developed country spends around 90 percent of their life indoors. So, despite the huge boom in health-based technology (fitness trackers, smartphone health apps, online fitness classes), it seems we're mostly trying to be healthy indoors, and usually while glued to a high-tech gadget.

But one of the best things we can do for our health involves using no screens, equipment, or technology whatsoever—just walking outside. We know how good we feel when we get some fresh air and go

for a walk. Walking in nature, rather than an urban environment, has been shown to improve mood and short-term memory in people with depression, as well as decrease the number of repetitive, negative thoughts and the type of brain activity associated with mental illness.

Stowing away your screens, putting down your phone, and going outside for a walk can't help but relax you! Using your walking time to think and appreciate your surroundings is mindfulness meditation at its most basic.

Take a dog, take a friend, or just take yourself—outside. Go for a walk.

———

2. Plant Something

—

Anyone who has spent time gardening understands just how therapeutic the experience can be—all the scents and sounds of the garden, and the sensory qualities of touching the plants, watering them, feeding them, and feeling soil on your hands.

Gardens are soothing spaces and tending to one is a rewarding pleasure. Working with plants can't be hurried and you can't garden with a phone in your hand either! But even if you don't happen to have a garden or access to a piece of land, you can still enjoy the sense of accomplishment that comes from when you nurture and grow something. A window box or even a single pot near some natural light is enough to grow a plant in. Watching something grow through the seasons connects us to the cycles of life and makes us feel renewed.

—

3. Look UP

—

When you walk down the street, what do you see? Do you notice anything beyond your phone screen and your feet? Would you be able to describe a building or statue that you pass every day on your way to work?

With our heads permanently buried in our screens we're losing the ability to appreciate the world around us. Today, when you're traveling between appointments in your day, make a conscious effort to look up and really notice what you see.

Challenge yourself to commit a building to memory, mentally noting every aspect of its architecture and appearance. Imagine that you will have to describe that building in detail to someone who will use it as a landmark on a route. Keep your eyes *up*.

You will probably find that with practice your observation skills will get better and that you'll know your way around your area a lot better too!

—

4. Go Cloud Spotting

—

You have lived under the same sky all your life. How long *is* that now? And how long since you last looked up at it?

Remember as a child when you used to stare at the sky, for what seemed like all day, trying to spot animals or funny face shapes in the clouds?

The beauty of the sky is that it's always there above our heads—we can access it at any time. And watching clouds drifting slowly across the sky, changing shape idly as they do, is one of the most relaxing and meditative experiences there is.

Go cloud spotting and see the sky with fresh eyes. It's entirely free (and screen-free) entertainment.

—

5. Sit in a Green Space

—

1. Step outside.

2. Walk to the nearest green space:
   your garden, a park, a small spot
   of grassy land nearby.

3. Sit right down on the grass.
   Not on a rock, or a bench, or a chair.

4. Feel the grass under your hands and
   feet. Drink in the sights, sounds,
   colors, and smells around you.

5. Breathe.

6. Take it all in.

7. And relax.

—

6. Cleanse

—

Throughout history we've sought out water for its restorative powers—"taking in the sea air" for all manner of ailments. But even if we live many miles away from the coast we can still seek out water wherever we are; rivers, canals, duck ponds, a water feature in a park—there's bound to be an expanse of water outside somewhere near you.

Find one. Sit down next to it and listen to the hypnotic sound of the water as it moves—whether that's waves crashing on a beach, a river flowing by, or water falling gently in a fountain.

Sit there for as long as you need. Emerge with your mind feeling cleansed.

—

For whatever we lose
(like a you or a me)
it's always ourselves
we find in the sea

E. E. CUMMINGS

7. Do Something Seasonal

—

Isn't it ironic that all the most popular screensavers and wallpapers are stunning shots of nature? We're staring at nature in all its beautiful forms every day on a screen to soothe us, instead of being out in it and feeling its power.

Shut away in our homes and offices we're losing track of the cycles of nature—the gentle movement through the seasons and all the subtle changes in the landscape. The

natural world is changing daily but when our heads are down, eyes glued to our screens, we don't even notice it happening. What a waste!

Go outside, and do something seasonal today to reconnect with the earth's cycle. Sit in a field of flowers in spring, wrap yourself in a blanket by a bonfire in autumn, go bird watching in the summer, or take part in a snowball fight in winter. Choose something that helps you appreciate the season you're in. Take part in your very own "screensaver" instead of looking at one.

———

8. Sleep Under the Stars

—

Our lives have become very small, limited by the tiny size of the screens we peer down at. Sometimes the whole world and everything that's important to us seems to be completely contained within the tiny rectangle of glass lying in our hands.

Staring up at the stars on a clear night opens our minds to the wonders of the natural world and our place in it. It can make us feel insignificant and small, but also shifts our awareness from obsessing over the smaller pieces of our lives to seeing how much more there is to the universe and its potential.

When you're struggling with just about anything, looking up on a starry night reminds you that we're all on the same planet, all struggling in the same way. It changes your perspective, expands your horizons, and quells your anxiety.

For a full immersion, grab a sleeping bag and sleep out under the canopy of stars, watching the lights fade and twinkle as the night passes. Nothing will seem so bad in the morning.

—

Look up at the stars, and not down at your feet. Try to make sense of what you see, and wonder about what makes the universe exist. Be curious.

STEPHEN HAWKING

TAME YOUR TRIGGERS

Technology is designed to be hard to ignore. Software engineers and app designers build in bells, whistles, banners, and badges to remind us, alert us, and keep us tethered to our screens.

These enticing sounds and sights trigger our automatic responses in a very primal way. Alerts, likes, and social media mentions spike dopamine levels in our brains, making us crave them more. And the unpredictable reward—we never know when a message or notification will arrive—makes us behave like addicts, unable to put our tech down for a much-deserved break.

Even when we set ourselves up with the best intentions, our tech can derail us. One study showed that just noticing a smartphone notification, even without responding to it, has a negative impact on focus, creativity, and problem solving.

The willpower to go digital-free is a muscle that needs exercising—and to help you build it up, this section has some tips on how to tame those common tech triggers.

1. Mute

—

As we're drowning amid a cacophony of communication, silence can be one of the hardest things to find in our digital-dominated world. But it's silence that combats the overstimulation we're all suffering from.

In silence we learn how important it is to let go of distractions. The absence of external voices puts us in touch with our inner voices. In silence we turn our attention to what's going on inside.

Set all your device notifications to silent. Shut off any vibrations and ring tones.

Do you notice how peaceful your world is when your technology isn't screaming at you for attention? And how much easier your screens are to ignore?

To extend the benefits, turn off all of your devices completely, find a quiet place, and sit in silence.

Shhhh.

—

Happiness is not found in things you possess, but in what you have the courage to release.

NATHANIEL HAWTHORNE

2. Declutter Your Digital Home

——

The acts of decluttering, tidying, and throwing things away have amazing therapeutic power. Clearing your home or work space and making way for new things helps you to identify what serves you best, and you can use the same decluttering techniques for your digital home screen as you do for your home.

Random apps are a good place to start. How many were downloaded and installed in a burst of enthusiasm and not used since? Be ruthless and go through all of the apps you haven't used in a while and uninstall or delete them.

Clear up your email inbox by deleting or filing all the messages that no longer need to be there. Delete old text-message threads. Prune your social-media feeds by unfollowing pages or people who no longer have a place in your life. Do the same with your contacts and address book.

Your newly decluttered digital home screen will entice you less, and serve you more.

——

3. Delay Your Response

———

According to a study of over two million email users, most emails are now answered in just two minutes.

Two minutes! How is it possible to get anything done if we're all responding so speedily? And yet we know how affronted we feel if our own messages aren't replied to quickly.

Faster response times are part of big cultural changes that happened when messaging and emailing took over our lives. The speed of technology encouraged us to start communicating in a very *particular* way—we started bashing our keys in rapid-fire replies, rather than taking time to pause and think about our responses.

We've bought into the idea that a fast response equals efficiency, but reacting instantly to emails and messages cuts through our thinking time on other tasks. And an ill-judged response can in fact tie us up in even more communication, wasting more time!

The constant stream of digital interruptions wrecks our concentration spans and ability to focus. Make a conscious effort to delay your response time to emails and messages that you know aren't urgent. Consider trying a system that has you only checking them once, or at most twice, a day to carve out thinking time for yourself. Set up an auto-responder if possible to let everyone know what you're doing and to manage expectations.

———

4. Go Off the Grid

—

It used to be that the restrictions on technology while traveling by plane meant that we could find some peace from the demands of our phones and devices. But with Wi-Fi becoming increasingly available in-flight, even that last precious sanctuary is disappearing.

But we are still left with a nifty little feature on our devices that we can make work for us at any time. Airplane mode is a useful way to keep your phone on and available but only when *you* decide to use it.

Whenever you need interruption-free time, make use of this helpful setting. Simply imagine that you're walking onto a plane. Turn your phone to airplane mode and put it away. Use that time to focus fully on what's happening in your life. Be there, not in that halfway world between your real life and your digital life.

Don't just wait for prompts from others to switch your phone to airplane mode, choose when to do it yourself too.

—

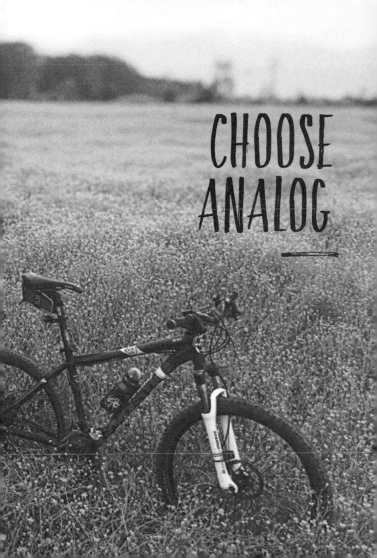

Sometimes new isn't always best. An age-old solution can be more efficient and more elegant than one that uses the latest technology. Writing by hand, for example, can be both aesthetically and tactilely pleasing; listening to music on vinyl often offers a greater sensual experience; and a great teacher can inspire more than any interactive app.

The digitization of books and art means we have a wealth of knowledge available at any time, which is easier to take for granted and not appreciate as much as we might if we held a physical book or saw an artwork in real life. What's more, some digital technologies, while saving us time, are stopping us from exercising our powerful mental abilities, such that we no longer attempt to remember phone numbers, addresses, times tables, or other frequently used information.

Who knows what the impact on our brains is as we stop using these skills? Technology when used as an aid strengthens us but when used as a crutch, can weaken us.

Digital technology has made our lives easier, but analog technologies make our lives richer and more rewarding. Quality of experience can win out over speed and efficiency. Challenging our brains to use our long-forgotten skills can surprise and delight us.

This section has a few reminders of real-world activities that are more fulfilling than the technological substitutes we've come to rely on instead.

1. Find Your Built-In GPS

O ur reliance on GPS and digital maps is reducing our natural ability to find our own way. Research indicates that when we use GPS we remember less about the places we go, and put less work into generating our own internal picture, or mental map, of the world.

Generating mental maps links to the development of other cognitive skills that may atrophy if we don't use them. If we can't navigate ourselves down a street without help, how can we ever hope to navigate the much more complicated terrain of our lives?

Strike out without a map and without GPS today. Choose a spot on the horizon and get yourself there, using only your own built-in navigational abilities. Rely on yourself and not your technology; get out of your comfort zone and see what you discover about yourself along the way.

2. Draw a Selfie

——

According to recent reports, an average twenty-something will take up to 25,700 selfies in their lifetime and around 93 million selfies are taken worldwide every day. Staggering!

But when we're snapping a selfie are we really seeing ourselves? Aren't we too busy calculating the right pose, and the right filter, to appreciate the unique contours and particular geometry of our faces? Selfies can make us harshly judgmental about our own appearances, rather than observant of them.

So take a long, hard look at yourself. Try drawing a selfie instead of snapping one.

Creativity in general can help put us in touch with our inner selves. Drawing our own faces especially is an exercise in understanding ourselves better. And if we are more in touch with ourselves then we can become more in touch with other people—the very opposite of our self-obsessed, selfie culture.

——

3. Think Positive

———

S ocial media makes us feel good. Likes trigger dopamine release, which fills us with a warm glow—no wonder some of us reload our social media feeds over and over again, to watch the likes building on our latest pictures or posts.

Think back for a moment to when you last received a real-world like—when someone paid you a compliment while looking at you face-to-face. Wasn't it so much more meaningful than seeing a little thumb, or a heart emoji, on a screen?

Take social media offline and hand out some real likes today.

Smile at a stranger and make them feel happy they encountered you during their day. Tell someone what you like about them, that they did something well, or simply how great they make you feel.

Social media should be echoing our real-world interactions, rather than replacing them. It makes such a difference when you show someone you care in person.

———

4. Just Ask

—

The internet is a wonderful thing. All those arguments settled by being able to immediately find out the answer! But having easy access to the "right" answers online means we've lost sight of the worth of asking for help from those around us.

Many of us fear not being good enough and so don't ask for help. But this can take us into a downward spiral of anxiety when we struggle to solve problems on our own using the internet, such as when obsessively googling a medical symptom.

We might feel we are burdening others if we ask—but you may be surprised how happy people are to help. We all know how good we feel when we can help, and by not asking others in return, we are depriving them of the same opportunity.

Reduce your reliance on the internet by reaching out and asking. Ask for directions on your way to somewhere new; ask your doctor instead of doing a digital diagnosis; ask for help with a tricky problem instead of fretting on your own. Just ask.

—

Asking for help with shame says: You have the power over me. . . . But asking for help with gratitude says: We have the power to help each other.

AMANDA PALMER

RECONNECT

Humans are social animals and we crave connection. With all of our many online friends, fans, and followers, it might seem like we have more connections than ever before. And yet, why do we feel so isolated sometimes?

Loneliness is on the rise, feelings of inadequacy are stirred up by witnessing our friends' "perfect" lives online, anxiety levels are soaring from the fear of missing out—the social media that was designed to bring us together can make us feel less connected, both to others and to ourselves.

The digital world can serve as a safety blanket for even the most socially confident. It creates a false sense of intimacy that stops us from going out and making connections in the real world. Sometimes it's just easier to hide behind a text, an email, or a photo comment than to meet or talk in real life. But by limiting our social relationships to purely digital ones, we're missing out on all the incredible benefits that come when we really connect with each other.

We need to disconnect from superficial online relationships, and reconnect with those that matter in the real world. This section has some suggestions on how to do just that.

1. Write a Postcard

Y ou don't have to be on vacation to send a postcard!

Postcards are like little rays of sunshine arriving in your mailbox. It only takes a few minutes to write and send one, but has a much longer-lasting impact on the recipient, who will enjoy it far more than reading a post made online instead.

Buy a pack of postcards.

Sit down and think of someone that you haven't been in touch with recently.

Write a simple message to let them know how you are, and that you've been thinking of them.

Attach a stamp, and send!

Repeat regularly with different recipients for maximum effect.

---

2. Talk More

—

M ost of us now use our smartphones more for texting than for talking. The very function the phone was designed for has become one of its least-used features. Text and email communication is exploding. In all age groups, every day, adults are texting and messaging each other far more than they are calling and talking to each other. Sometimes we're even messaging people in the same room!

But just because messaging is easier and quicker doesn't mean we should default to it. Text or email messages to apologize and explain may be far less uncomfortable than an encounter in person or by phone, but written words can't reflect the warmth of a tone of a voice, or the unmistakable sincerity that comes from eye contact.

Make a decision to type less, and to talk more. Weigh up each piece of communication and judge whether some might be better delivered in person, or possibly via a phone call. More than that,

strike up a conversation with someone you don't usually talk to: a sales clerk, someone on your commute, or an elderly neighbor for example.

Rediscover the power of talking to strengthen or make a connection today.

—

3. Friend Someone

—

Do you find yourself measuring your worth by how many online friends you have? The ease of clicking on someone's name, and asking him or her to be your friend, harks back to the playground in its simplicity. But although maintaining friendships online is a great way of keeping in touch with people you can't see in person more frequently, it's no substitute for spending time with friends in real life.

Friendships are messy and complicated but always repay the amount of time put into them. And as we get older our circle of friends can narrow as we stop putting in the effort that we made to strike up new friendships when we were younger.

Make a resolution to make a new friend. Maybe someone you vaguely know from a fitness class, or a colleague you haven't been able to spend much time with. Invite them for coffee or lunch or to an activity with you. It's a much slower process than simply sending an online friend request, but if you put in the effort, you'll reap far greater rewards.

—

4. Write a Secret Note

—

One of the most addictive qualities of the digital world has its roots in what psychologists call "unpredictable rewards." Because we don't know when the next text, email, message, or like will arrive, we find ourselves compulsively checking our smartphones and screens for the dopamine rush we experience when we do get one.

Receiving something when you're not expecting it is a singular pleasure. The idea that someone was thinking about you at the precise moment that they sent it makes you feel happy.

You can go one better in the offline world by writing and hiding a secret note to someone you love, live with, or work with. Nothing complicated, just a scrap of paper with a handwritten message to say, "I love you," "Well done!" or even just "Hi!" and sign off so that they know it's from you when they find it!

To maximize its impact, hide the note somewhere completely unexpected. The more creative and surprising your hiding place the better. It's far rarer to find a secret note than to receive a text, so you're going to give the recipient a pretty powerful dopamine rush! And it will make you feel good too.

———

5. Play the Game

—

There is probably a particular screen-based game that you are fond of: it seems a different one is launched every day that sweeps the world up into a new viral frenzy.

But if we're toiling on screens all day at work and then unwinding by playing on screens too, there's no respite for our tired brains and sore eyes.

Board games are an escape. They're great screen-free home entertainment, and far more sociable than screens as they nearly all require several real-life players.

Make a list of board games you enjoyed as a child. You may even have some still lingering at the back of a closet. Cajole and bribe friends and family to take part in a board game evening. Ask each of them to bring a game they enjoy too. You may discover a new game to add to your list of favorites and you will definitely have a fun screen-free evening.

—

You must live in the present, launch yourself on every wave, find your eternity in each moment. Fools stand on their island opportunities and look toward another land.

HENRY DAVID THOREAU

6. Be Present

—

Our time is precious and limited, and yet we're wasting so much of it every day. We now spend more time on our screens than we do sleeping, and so much of it is the mindless screen scrolling we do to distract ourselves when we feel uncomfortable or bored.

Every day we reject an experience or a relationship in favor of time with our screens. Our loved ones feel ignored and resentful that our phones and screens get to spend more time with us than they do.

Giving our time and attention is the most precious thing we can give. Better than any gift-wrapped box or bunch of flowers.

If there is just one thing you do as result of reading this book, let it be this: give your full attention to everyone you're with. Put down your phone, put away your screens, and focus on the person you're with in the moment, unreservedly.

Be present. Don't split your attention with a screen. And witness every relationship and connection grow richer.

—

Acknowledgments

—

With grateful thanks to Zara Anvari at Octopus who had the vision for this book and the confidence that I could write it. To Francesca Leung for all her hard work editing and to Megan van Staden for a design that reflects the spirit of my words perfectly.

To Sarah Graveling who helped me create the Time To Log Off brand (as well as every other brand I have ever launched) and who always makes something beautiful out of my jumble of ideas.

To Andrew Syer for prompting me to shape my philosophy and find my voice.

To Tessa and Ron Short for their support always.

To Clare Awdry, Yashodha Balraj, Emily Cowan, Lisa Day, Sophie Hanscombe, Jackie Jones, Sophie Lewisohn, Tracy Northampton, Ros O'Neill, Anna Paolozzi and Ronke Phillips for love, food, excellent style, words of encouragement, and keeping me sane while I was juggling writing this book with the rest of my life.

To Al Mackinnon who introduced me to a different way of looking at the world, and who inspired me to set off on my digital detox journey.

—